BUILDING FAITH

BUILDING FAITH

BETTY HINER-PICKENS
Michael Hiner

Superior Publishing LLC.

CONTENTS

Dedication vi

1. Where Is Your Faith? 1
2. Abounding Love 8
3. Individual Plea 14
4. Trust 21
5. His Hands 27
6. Conclusion: Choices 32

About The Author 37

Thanking God for His grace, mercy, deliverance, and forgiveness.

To my sons:

Michael and Kenneth Hiner, you two are very important to me.

God is working on you both, to make you the men He wants you to be. And this is a great deal to me. No matter how you mess up, God still forgives and He will love us no matter what but we have to give ourselves to Him.

Copyright © 2024 by Betty Hiner-Pickens

ISBN/SKU978-1-953056-48-1
EISBN978-1-953056-50-4

All rights reserved. No part of this book may be reproduced in any manner whatsoever without written permission except in the case of brief quotations embodied in critical articles and reviews.

Superior Publishing LLC, 2024
(662)295-9893

CHAPTER 1

Where Is Your Faith?

We are living in troublesome times. Is there anything that can be done as far as change is concerned? Does any hope lie ahead? How can I make a difference? These are questions I find myself asking.

First, before we start, I think it is very important that we look at the word hope. The word hope, to me, is a sense of longing for things to come, whether good or bad. Now, we all long for things that are good because God is good, and everything He made is good. But before you do anything, you have first got to believe in Him. Believe that God exists. That's where faith comes in. It is believing or hoping in things unseen. Seeing is not believing, but believing is seeing. Just because you can't see the air doesn't stop you from breathing. Furthermore, just because you can't see God doesn't stop you from believing. That's what we call faith. For Hebrews 11:1 says, Now faith is the substance of things hope for; the evidence of things not seen. Also, faith comes by hearing, and hearing by the word of God, that's Romans 10:17.

Often times, it's hard to stay focused, think positive, or even keep the faith especially when you can't see the sunshine when there always seems to be a storm in the midst. I couldn't see the light at the end of the tunnel, so to speak, so I began to read my Bible and talk to God more.

You see, I confessed hope in Christ at an early age. I was mentored by my pastor. I became very active in church. I sang in the choir, taught Sunday school, and worked with various organizations. I thought that by being active in the church was all it took to be saved. I knew the Lord and what He could do, but I never let go so God could take control.

All during my life, while continuing to work in the church, I soon found out that I didn't know Christ like I thought. What I mean is, I knew Christ was real, but in order for him to work in my life, a change had to take place. You see, I did things, and I knew that they were wrong. I prayed and asked for forgiveness but continued to fall into the temptations of the world. I never put forth any effort to really change. All these things had become a way of life for me, a habit or an addiction you might say.

My conscience, the Holy Spirit, made my sins known, but I paid no attention. One Sunday during service, I received a huge awakening. The pastor asked this question, and I quote,"If you were to die today, where would your soul spend eternity?"

That question began to bother me. I had no idea as to where my soul would spend eternity. I didn't feel that it would be heaven. I knew that I was in trouble. I knew that tomorrow wasn't promised. I knew that I had to make a change. My talk, my walk had to be different. A major change had to occur in my physical life in order for me to be able to grow and prosper in my spiritual life. All during this time in my life, God kept me. I'm very blessed and truly grateful that He saw something in me worth saving. He has and still is forgiving me over and over again for all my wrongdoings and disobedience.

I became determined to make a change. One day while sitting alone, I began to flip through the channels. I stopped on a religious broadcast. A preacher was speaking, and he said these words,

"It's time to let go and let God. Step out on faith and watch God work!" But worldly influences continued to surface on every hand. The pressure was ever so great.

One Easter Sunday, while attending a singing at church, I saw how happy, how full of the Spirit a family member of mine was. I didn't only see this in her at church, but at work and in her home. No matter what came her way, she always seems to have joy. I remember thinking to myself, I want some of that, joy that is.

While at the singing, she seemed to just know that I was wrestling with something. She turned to me and said these words, "Now is a good time. Go on."

The Spirit was high and my heart was really heavy. But I knew that I wanted some good, some joy in my life for once. At that very moment, I made up in my mind that I was going to do just that. After all, what did I have to lose? I gave my life to Christ, and I have been running for him ever since. I'm a sinner saved by grace, but I'm saved. Romans 10:9 says, "That if thou confess with thy mouth and believe in thine heart thou shalt be saved."

Now don't get me wrong, I'm still faced with trouble and opposition everyday. There are even times that the human side surface and I fall. But the Holy Spirit is there to convict me of all my wrong. Therefore, I pray and ask for forgiveness for my sins known and unknown. For the Bible says if you confess your sins to Him, He is faithful and just to forgive you and cleanse you from all wrong, 1John 1:9. My God is a just and forgiving God. Also, confession is good for the soul. Once you confess and truly ask for forgiveness, the Holy Spirit will not condemn you.

I used to beat myself up over the wrong I did, not knowing how to forgive myself. From reading my bible, prayer, and talking with a close family member, I have learned how to forgive myself. Things that I was bothered by, home, work, church, I can truly say are becoming worries of the past. I have learned that in order to grow spiritually, you have got to love and forgive one another, even forgive yourself.

I stepped out on faith and gave God my hand. He took the wheel and now He is in control. I try to walk and live in a way that will lead me to His marvelous light. With the guidance of the Holy spirit, I pray for help to avoid and ignore worldly influences that are still present in many different forms. Everything the devil took, God is giving it all back to me. For once, I can truly finally say, I know who

I am, and I know whose I am. It took me a while to get to that point, it wasn't easy, but by the grace of God, I made it. I am beginning to have joy and peace inside like I have never known. I'm so thankful that someone prayed for me. I'm thankful to God that he never left me. Jesus is the living water. It is by His grace and mercy that the blood He shed for me, saved me. I have come this far by God's grace through faith. He changed my life and now I'm complete. And one day, I hope to sit at His feet.

That's why I decided to write this book called, Building Faith. James 2:26 says,"Faith without works is dead. Also, works without faith is dead."

Again remember Romans 10:17, "Faith comes by hearing and hearing by the word of God. Salvation is free. God paid the price a long time ago with His life. But a step-by-step walk with God will lead you to the light.

My God is a jealous God. God has done so much for us. Take time and give Him the highest praise! Be persistent in your praise. Praise God at the coming up of the sun and the going down of the same. Praise the Lord while you are still above ground because when you are waxed cold, you won't be able to make a sound. Lift your eyes to the hills from whence comes all your help, for your help comes from the lord, Psalms 121:1.

Stand tall, don't fall, come on and praise the Lord. Seek the Lord while He may be found. For the Lord is our Shepherd say Psalms 23. Man looks at the outside, but God looks at the heart. Don't let man decide you're fate. His power, His love, His Amazing Grace is all one needs. Know the truth, spread the truth for it is the truth that will make you free. You can search the whole world over and never find anybody like Jesus. Cuz Can't Nobody Do you like the Lord.

Memorize these words:
I'm a conqueror; I'm victorious, I won't be stopped!
I'm an achiever; I'm a believer, I won't be blocked!
God made us who we are. We are his masterpiece.
Step out on faith. Try him today. He won't let you down.

Prayer:
Thank You Master for seeing something in me worth saving. Please help me to adhere to your will. Fill me with the Holy Spirit, I pray. Help me to live a life that is pleasing in thy sight. Dear Lord, as long as the blood runs warm in my vein, I will try and give you praise. And when I fall, help me to be humble to admit my sin and say I'm sorry, please forgive me. In Jesus name I pray. Amen.

Here are some inspiring scriptures on faith:

Hebrews 11:1
Now Faith is a substance of things hoped for, the evidence of things not seen.
1 Corinthians 4:2
Now it is required that those who have been given a trust must prove faithful.
Psalms 117:2

For great is His love toward us, and the faithfulness of
the Lord endures forever.
2 Corinthians 5:7
For we walk by faith and not by sight.

Food for the soul:
Where focus goes, energy flows.

Life's little recipe:
Fill your future with possibilities by letting Jesus have
His way, believe and never doubt, pray everyday.

CHAPTER 2

Abounding Love

You know, love is an action word. At times, in all our lives, it gets very hard to show love. Especially, when you reach out and give and give, and it all seems to be in vain. Everything you do to try and help to make things better for someone, and they turn around, disrespect you and tell you right to your face that you are not trying to help them, or that you don't even care about them. Words hurt. Whoever told you that they don't, told a lie. It gets hard to look over it. It makes you just want to throw up your hands and be done. But as children of God, we have to "PUSH." Pray until something happens. We have to keep on loving in spite of. Love is a sacrifice. That's why we should let the love of Christ abound in us.

You see, what the world needs now is love. Yes, the world needs pure, genuine, sweet love. If, in the hearts of man, everyone will start to live a life that portrays true, real faith, then we would see and experience this true genuine love that we hear and read about. It won't be perfect by no means. After all, there was only one that came who was perfect. But we will see signs of imperfection begin to change. A change for the better for all mankind.

My Father in Heaven is a never changing God. He's the same today as He was yesterday and will be forevermore. Jesus is the example of what true love and perfect peace should be. Satan knows your name, but he calls you by your sin for he comes only to rob, kill, and destroy. God, on the other hand, knows your sin, but He calls you by your name. That's love.

He would never leave nor forsake you. His love can't be beat. The Lord is true, He's real, He's unconditional. He can't be bought. There's nothing, no job, or any amount of money that will ever equal or be worth more than anything that God has or is doing for man. Nothing will ever compare to His love. St John 3:16 says, For God so loved the world that He gave His only begotten Son that whosoever believeth in Him should not perish but shall have everlasting life. Now tell me, who wouldn't serve a God like that?

God doesn't make us do things to get His way. His love doesn't work that way. He only asks of us. He asked that we love one another just as He loves us. He asked us to spread His word. He tells us to ask for forgiveness for our wrongdoings, and He wants us to try and live holy. God is a just and caring God. He knows that we're going to make mistakes and even fall sometimes. But that's okay. When deception came in, we received what was ugly-sin. We were born into a world of sin therefore that makes us all sinners. Accept it, but just know you don't have to stay that way. It doesn't matter how you fall or even what causes you to fall, it's how you get up. Don't give up and don't give in. Realize the problem, admit it, and give it to God. Ask for forgiveness and strength to hold on and wait on the Lord. After all, He's there for all who seek Him. Call Him by His name. His love is never ending. Trust and believe. Try Him and see what He can do. Through endurance and encouragement from the word, there is hope. For blessed is the man who trust in the Lord, who's trust is the Lord says Jeremiah 17:7. For God gave us a spirit not of fear, but of power, love, and self-control. Be still and watch the power of God's love come down.

There are numerous accounts and events mentioned in the Bible of long ago that portrays the power and love of God. Here are just a few. The three Hebrew boys in the fiery furnace, they trusted God, kept the faith, and God delivered them. Also, there was a woman with the issue of blood. She believed that just by touching the hem of His garment, she would be made whole. Because of her unwavering faith, the Lord healed her. In addition, there is Noah and the ark, Daniel in the Lion's den, the feeding of the multitude. Even our Lord Himself had to overcome evil by continuing to trust in His Heavenly Father. The book called, the Bible, is where all these stories and more can be found. Set aside a little time, sit down, and begin to read God's word. I can assure you, you won't be disappointed. His love doesn't stop there though, His love and His power is still available today, the same way it was way back then. Now is the time to give God a try. Step out on faith, and you won't go wrong.

God is omnipresent. He died a sinner's death. He laid in the sinner's tomb. He's the only one who doesn't have a skeleton in a closet. Our Lord is the only one who doesn't have a skeleton in a coffin. God's love is true, it's real, it's unconditional. Simply put, here's words to a song I wrote titled-"HE'S UNCONDITIONAL."

"He's a joy to know. He's caring and forgiving everywhere He goes. It was on the cross where He paid the cost. For me, no love, no love, was lost. He may not come when you want, but He's always on time. Trust and believe, for comfort in Him you will find. Weeping may endure for a night, but joy comes with the morning light. There is no doubt in my mind, He's one of a kind. His grace and mercy set me free. Without Him, I don't know where I would be. For me He died and now in Him my soul abides."

God's love is not a prenup. It's a bond of unity. It covers a multitude of sin. God's love is a sure and steadfast anchor for our soul. It loves in spite of and regardless of. Because of His love for us, despite of our ugliness and waywardness, He outstretched his arms and died for you and me. That's real, true unconditional love. His love has been poured into our hearts through His Holy Spirit in which He is in the midst. He will quieten us by His love. Let it rule and supersede over everything in your life.

Now I asked you, what are you willing to do for His love? Are you ready to experience, enjoy, and become a part of His amazing love? If so, step out. Put your faith into action. Do it today. God takes pride in loving us. We ought to take pride in serving him.

Prayer:
Dear Lord, thank You for your abounding love that you spread from above.
Thank you for Your amazing grace that You see something in me worth saving.
I thank You for the chance to grow and beautify the seeds that I sow.
Thank You for giving me something to look forward to.
For everything brings about something new.
In Jesus name.
Here are a few scriptures on love:
Romans 8:28
And we know that for those who know God, all things work together for good for those who are called according to His purpose.

Ephesians 4:2
Be completely humble and gentle; be patient, bearing with one another in love.

1 Peter 4:8
Above all, love each other deeply because love covers a multitude of sins.

1 Corinthians 13:4-8

Love is patient and kind, loves does not envy or boast, it is not arrogant or rude. It does not insist on its own way; it is not irritable or resentful, it does not rejoice in wrong-doings, but rejoices with the truth. Love bears all things, believes all things. Love never ends.

St John 3:16
For God so love the world that He gave His only begotten Son that whosoever believeth in Him should not perish but she'll have everlasting life.

1 John 4:19
We love because he first loved us.

Food for the soul:
God is holding the receipt; where would we be, if he redeemed it?

Life's little recipe:
One part prayer; two parts patience; three parts a devotion a day will keep the devil away. What more can I say?

CHAPTER 3

Individual Plea

It's me again. I feel that everyone that knows Christ should do a personal inventory of one's self. That is, a self-check of the good and bad aspects of self. Now, we know that we all have some good and bad in us. That's okay. But we should want the good to outweigh the bad. That's why I believe that it is good for everyone to have an individual plea. An appeal or request to God for oneself. My individual plea is to be an all around good and faithful human being. Now, I'm not perfect. I fall the same as all of you. But by knowing Christ, I've learned how to ask for forgiveness and try to live Holy. Now, I don't say much to many people. Some people even say that I am mean because I don't associate with many people. That doesn't make me mean just careful I think. And I've learned not to let what people say and think about me, bother me. I just be me. God made me and I'm proud.

One thing we need to realize is that on this road we call life, the journey is not going to be easy. People are going to misuse you, mistreat you, even abuse you. Some of these people will be ones you know, trust, and even love. I come to tell you, it's only your test. The Lord said to be strong and of good courage in Deuteronomy 31:6. Man has neither a heaven or hell in which to put you. Don't retaliate or fight back. The battle is not yours, it's the Lord's says, 2 Chronicles 20:15. Don't let the devil steal your joy. Keep the faith. Help is here, and He's here to stay.

But activation of faith has to start with self. One must see self for who they really are and not for what they think or want to see. Also, once you ask God to make him or her who or what he would have them to be. Ask and it shall be given, seek and you shall find, knock and it shall be opened unto you. Matthew 7:7. The Bible says we are all transgressors, but God can fix us if we let Him. He can and will change you, but you have to become willing and accessible. Open yourself to God and allow Him to come in. Move self out of the way, and allow Him to do His will. Work on me should be your plea!

God is not a joke. Activation of true faith is a must. God's visions and perceptions are totally different from man's. One must have that unwavering faith in order to accept what God is doing. Also, while God is working, you have got to be patient. The transformation is not going to happen overnight mind you, but be still and allow God to fulfill His will.

Some may have counted you out, but don't lose hope. We all stumble. Isaiah 40:30 says, "Even the youth shall faint and be weary and the young men shall utterly fall, and they that wait on the Lord shall renew their strength." So don't quit, for hope of the righteous does not put us to shame, but brings joy. Hold fast to the confession of your hope. Pray for strength. Start by asking God to be your God. God's love is faithful. Christ is Faithful over God's house as a Son, and we are his house, if indeed we hold fast to our confidence and boasting in hope.

We can never repay the debt, but God believes we are all worth it. For our work of faith, labor of love, and steadfastness of hope in the Lord will bring us through. For whoever lives in love, lives in God and God in them. That's why we should seek His face. Get to know His name. Experience the power of His love. The race is not given to the swift, but to the one who endures to the end, Ecclesiastes 9:11.

If you are tired of losing battles, give your life to God. My God always looks out for His own. You are not trash. We are all gifts from God. Yes, you may be a diamond in the rough. Nothing ever seems to go right. But God's chemical laboratory of redemption can change all of that. God designed you to sparkle and shine, but don't shine so others can see you; shine so that through you, others can see God. If you bring yourself down a notch, God will lift you up. God is your deliverer. Regardless of situations, even when you stumble, remember to give God the praise. Don't worry about what people think or say for when you are righteous, the life you live will speak for you. Know and be proud that you are a diamond in the rough because God is not through with you yet. Come on and get fired up for the Lord. Do it today!

This brings me to another song I wrote titled, "Get Fired Up." It goes something like this:

"Give your life to the Lord; allow Him to do His will. He will clean you from the inside out, for His love is really real. When your journey is completed, and to God, you have been true; if by earthly friends forsaken, He'll be right there for you.
Get fired up for the Lord. Why not do it today. Get inspired and taste of the goodness of the Lord."

Ask yourself these questions: First, am I solid in my faith? Second, is the type of life I live in obedience or according to God's will? Also, am I committed to obeying and following the will of God? Believe God when no one else does. There are benefits to serving God. Remember, I said previously to push, "pray until something happens" because there will be times in our lives that our needs will become so great and our resources so limited, that our worship will become our only pleading for God's intervention in our troubled lives or the lives of those dear to us. That's why it's important to keep your conversation with God going. God may seem dead to your pleading, but don't stop pleading or praying because, if nothing else, at least you are still in conversation with the Lord. When life gives you more than you can stand, just kneel. Even when the way seems dark and things seem impossible trust and believe. Keep the faith. God hears you and without faith it is impossible to please him like it says in Hebrews 11:6.

This is your season. It's the perfect time to let go and let God. God can and will turn things around for you. He'll reach way down and pick you up. He will take out the old and put in the new. For David says in the bible,"Create in me a clean heart." Ask God to do it. Then, believe and watch God take you from a lack of faith and disappointment, to a place of peace and contentment. With God as your leader, if He brings you to it, He will bring you through it. With God by your side, everything may not work out the way you want, but it will work out for your good. God is using all of your experiences, both good and bad, to develop your character to match your calling.

    Reach out for your blessings. The battle is in your mind. Your mind is a garden. Your thoughts are the seeds. Listen, believe, and trust. God should not be your last resort. He should be your first resource. God is not the one with the problem of giving. We are the ones with the problem of receiving. Remember God lives in all of us in spite of the condition of our hearts or lives. You are the master of your future. You are the captain of your soul. You can't change your past, but you can choose your destiny. God is the only one who can change your past. For the Bible say, John 14:6 "That Jesus is the way, the truth, and the light;no man comes unto the Father but by me. Time is running out. Lighten up, let Him surface. Believe Him! Accept Him! Try Him today! Give God your heart and watch him give you a new start. Take the plunge. Be the change you wish to see in the world today.

Prayer:

Dear Lord, we need You. Lord we want you.

Father in Heaven, we desire You. Holy Spirit, please make your presence known. Dear Lord, please begin in me. In Jesus name. Amen.

A few inspiring scriptures on spiritual evaluation and pleas:

1 Corinthians 11:28

But a man must examine himself, and in so doing he is to eat of the bread and drink of the cup.

2 Corinthians 13:5

Examine yourself as to whether you are in the faith. Test yourselves. Can't you see for yourselves that Jesus Christ is in you unless you actually fail the test.

Job 16:21

On behalf of a man he pleads with God, as a man pleads for his neighbor.

Psalms 140:6

So I say to the Lord, You are my God, listen to my voice as I plead for mercy, Lord.

Food for the soul:

Inhale your future; exhale your past.

Life's little recipe:

Trying to win a fight will take all night; but if we flee, we shall be free.

Attitude equals altitude; for prayer, patience, and perseverance is all you need.

CHAPTER 4

Trust

If you are tired of being the same; tired of things not changing, step out on faith and give it your best shot. The walk may be rough. The climb may be hard, but don't give up. Pain and trials come to make us strong. God knows that we cannot make this journey alone. He knows that we cannot get right by ourselves. That's why he sent us power from on high. His name is Jesus. He's there for all who seek Him. God sees what man can't. His visions and provisions are totally different from ours. The love you need, He already gave. Getting close to Jesus doesn't mean you won't have storms in your life, but the closer you get to Jesus the more peace you will have. There's hope in the word.

You must have that unwavering faith in order to accept what He is doing. Even though the transformation may not happen overnight, be still and allow God to fulfill His will. Isaiah 40:31 says, "They that wait on the Lord shall renew their strength; they shall mount up on wings as eagles. They shall run and not be weary; they shall walk and not faint." Nothing will change if you expect more of the same, believe and watch God take you from a lack of faith and disappointment, to a place of peace and contentment. Get excited about your future. Start expecting God's goodness. Ask God to be your guide. With God as your leader, if He brings you to it, He will bring you through it. With God by your side, everything may not work out the way you want it, but it will work out for your good and when God gets through, oh what a great change it will be.

God's love is faithful. Christ is also faithful over his father's house as a son, and we are God's house, if we indeed hold fast our confidence and boasting in hope. God is our strength. Psalms 28:7 says the Lord is my strength and my shield. My heart trust in Him and He helps me.

It only takes a little faith. The faith the size of a mustard seed. After all, prayer is the key and faith unlocks the door. For 1Thessalonians 5:17, says pray without ceasing, for the prayers of the righteous availeth much. Little prayer, little power; much prayer, much power; no prayer, no power.

Prayer is a lifestyle not an emergency exit. Prayer is the world's greatest wireless connection. Jesus hears your tears like prayers, and our tears come to make us stronger. When you can't put your prayers into words, God hears your heart. No matter how you pray, with words or emotions, when prayers go up, blessings come down.

It is not where you start. It is where you land that matters. Put your trust in Him. Test your faith. Be bigger than your fear. Believe and watch God open the windows of heaven and pour you out a blessing. One of Satan's greatest fears is prayer with an intercessor. The Bible says that when two or three gather in my name there I am also, Matthew 18:20.

Here are just a few ways I have found that help me to trust and step out on faith. First, admit that you are a sinner. Confess your faults one to another. Believe that Jesus gave His life for you like it says in John 3:16. Next, ask God to forgive you for all your wrongdoings. When you do wrong, tell God you are sorry and apologize to those you have wronged.

Be persistent in your prayers. "PUSH" means pray until something begins to happen. Just know that when God says no, it is not a rejection but a redirection. But when Jesus says yes, nobody can say no. Keep praying whether you understand or not. Delay answers to our prayers teach us to give it to God. It moves us from place of doubt and fear to a place of belief and trust. Be patient and wait until He gives you a new direction.

Furthermore, adhere to the voice of the Holy Spirit. Stop and listen to what the Lord has to say. God knows where the emergencies come in our lives. He will never lead you wrong.

Don't put your trust on delay. Delayed obedience brings about disobedience. The instruction you follow determines the future you create. Putting your faith on layaway will only cancel what God has for you. Put it on the now. Where there is a vision, with faith, there is provision. Expect something good today.

In addition, give your life to Christ. Ask God to take control, that way, when you fall, it won't be hard to say sorry and ask for forgiveness. Take a step of obedience. Do it today. Don't let this opportunity pass you by. Finally know that salvation is free, and it's because of God's Amazing Grace that we are still here. God is a balance keeper. Trusting Him is the key. He can heal every hurt in your heart. He's mind over matter. Trust Him. Believe Him. Put Him to the test. Exercise your faith and watch God work it out.

Only the strong survive. God Is watching over you. I know because I asked Him to. He is the only one who can fill a void. Come to Him right now. He wants to save you. According to Matthew 11:28 in the Bible, it says come to me all you who are heavy laden, and I will give you rest. He wants to give you salvation.

Hope says God can; faith says God will. For faith tells me that, no matter what lies ahead of me, God is already there. Where there is hope, there is faith; where there is faith, there lies miracles. You never know how God will use you until you let Him. What will you trust him for today?

Prayer:
Lord help me not to ask why, but to put my trust in you to work it out.
Help me to lean on you and not let go. In Jesus name.
Amen.

Some inspiring scriptures on trust:

Psalms 9:10

Those who know your name trust in you, for you, Lord have never forsaken those who seek you.

Psalms 13:5
But I trust your unfailing love. My heart rejoices in your salvation.

Psalms 56:3
When I am afraid I put my trust in you.

Proverbs 3:5
Trust in the Lord with all your heart, and lean not until thy own understanding. In all thy ways acknowledge Him, and He shall direct thy path.

Romans 15:13
May the God of hope fill you with all joy and peace as you trust in Him, so that you may overflow with hope by the power of the Holy Spirit.

Psalms 37:5
Commit your way to the Lord trust Him, and He will act.

Food for the soul:
When in life you seem to be drowning, remember your lifeguard walks on the water.

Life's Little Recipe:

If life throws you a curve ball; push on, do not quit, ask God to redirect your swing, then step into the pitch.

CHAPTER 5

His Hands

God wants people that are real, not actors, for His army. Get acquainted with Him. The only way to know Him is through reading His word, fasting, and praying.

God's hands are not short. He is not a guy that He should lie. God's hands can change any man. He can make any wrong right, your crooked road straight. He's not a respecter of persons. What He did for others, He will do for you. He's standing with arms wide open. What more do you need? Activate your faith. Do it today.

Again, the word of God says in Matthew 18:20 that when two or three Gather in the name of Jesus, there He is also. There is comfort in God's hands. Your relationship with God is in God's hands, but your fellowship with the Lord is in your hands. You can't have fellowship with God unless you have fellowship with Jesus, the Son.

We forget sometimes about the I too. We all have sinned and fallen short. No matter what you say or do to someone, at the end of the day, they are still human. We all are a work in progress.

God wants us to reevaluate ourselves. First, we need to deny self. The needs of others should come first. Next, make sure Christ is first in your thoughts, decisions, and actions. Life is not a burger king. You can't have it your way always. Everyone has value. We all are at different stages in our life. We all forget sometimes where we have come from. But if we remain in Christ, we will always come back to that root. God made us all with His hands; and therefore, everyone has some worth.

The Lord says come unto me all that are heavy laden, and I will give you rest in Matthew 11:28. My Father in Heaven is just waiting for you to invite Him in. Be alert to pressure. God warns us to be careful of the doings of the devil. For he comes to rob, kill, and destroy. Put on the whole armor of God says, Ephesians 6:11. Become fully equipped by reading the word, fasting, and praying.

Knowledge comes from the word. Wisdom comes from knowledge, and all comes from God. Jesus does not respond to sin. He responds to the word. God will never ask you for something you don't have. He will ask you for something you want to keep. Don't give up something that you have mastered that is good. Ask to give up something that has mastered you.

In other words, rest in his promise. God will treat you better than you treat yourself. What you won't do for yourself, God will do. Nothing is easier to replace than money; but nothing is harder to replace than uncommon favor with

God. The Bible is the greatest book of wisdom that God gives in making decisions. His word filters our thinking and desires when we are not right. When reading the word, God sifts and builds our faith. Just be patient and wait.

We have victory and power in Jesus. In other words, when you become a blessing to others, God will become a blessing to you. What you make happen for others, God will make happen for you. And, what you do for others, God will do the same for you. Just make sure that what you do is for the good of all that is involved.

God will never circumvent authority. The responsibility of obedience is up to you, but the responsibility of blessings is up to God. The anointing of the Holy Spirit, given to you, is a sign that shows God will make great things happen for you. God is a God of all harvest. He is the planter. The world is the field. We are the seeds, and the devil is the enemy. The Harvesters are God's angels, and the Harvest time is Judgment day. What you sow will bring the Harvest, but if you don't sow anything, don't expect a harvest. Luke 6:38 says give and it shall be given unto you. A good measure pressed down, shaking together, and running over will be poured into your lap. For the good measure you use, it will be measured to you. In other words, give of yourself. It matters not how much. Give what you have, and God will reward you plenty. Great is thy reward my good and faithful servant says the Lord in Matthew 5:12.

Thy reward will be a seat in the Kingdom of Heaven. The Kingdom of Heaven is so big that the devil will never be able to overtake it. We will rest in Heaven if we do what we are supposed to do while here on Earth. The reminder of judgment is to make sure we are working because we are in the fold and there is still work to be done.

This day is a gift from God. Hearts are starting to beat again. Dreams are coming alive. Passions are being restored. Recognize your gift. Stir It up. Get ready for God's goodness. Get ready for His favor. Be happy with what He has to give. Accept it with all your heart. For your greatest victory is in your future.

Prayer:
Dear Lord thank You for holding me in Your arms, and being a fence all around me. Thank You for constantly keeping me by Thy grace and tender mercy. In Jesus name.
Amen.

A few scriptures on God's hands:
Acts 7:50
Was it not my hands which made all things?

Psalms 89:13
You have a strong arm. Your hand is my mighty; Your right hand is exalted.

Psalms 19:1
The Heavens are telling of the Glory of God. And their expanse is declaring the works of His hands.

Isaiah 64:8

But now, oh Lord, You are our Father we are the clay.
And you are our Potter. And all of us are the works of your hands.

Food for the soul:
God's heart is touched by our needs, but God's hands are touched by our seeds.

Life's Little Recipe:
Don't set your mind on the flesh, for it leads to death. But set your mind on the Spirit. It brings life and peace. Everyday may not be a good day, but there is some good in every day. Let go and let God. He's only a prayer away.

CHAPTER 6

Conclusion: Choices

Life with Jesus is sweet. It is not because we are good but because God is good. People will come and people will go, but Jesus will remain forever.

But serving the Lord requires the renewal of choice. You have a chance to sow good or bad seeds. Those are the ones that are going to sprout. Good seeds will be rewarded, but bad seeds will perish.

Keep your eyes on the prize says Hebrew 12:2, which is the high calling of the Lord. For the prize is God, and the reward is Heaven. The Kingdom of Heaven has an open door. No man can shut it. Only God has that power. Everyone has a chance to get in. But works alone can't save you. You need to make sure you are in the number cause it will be those that are in the number that will get in. It's just like going to a club, restaurant, concert, etc. without being in that number, no ticket, no reservation, you can't get in. You may plead and beg all you want, but if you're not in that number, there will be no acceptance or any exceptions.

Jesus is on His way back, it's time out for Mr. Rogers in the neighborhood. Allow Jesus in the neighborhood. The neighborhood should begin in you. We want to reap the benefits, but don't want to put in the work. I come to tell you; no work, no benefits. If you haven't done as God asked you to do during your life and ask for forgiveness when you fall and make a change, you won't get up and you won't get in.

It's time to make a choice. Decisions are the hardest things to make especially when it is a choice between where you should be and where you want to be. Matthew 6:24 says a man can't serve two masters. You are free to make whatever choice you want, but you are not free from the consequences of the choice.

The choices we make have a major impact on the life we live. Make the right choices on a daily basis that you may live a life that is true to who you want to be, and who you want to belong to. It's time to make a choice. Where do you want your soul to spend eternity? Heaven and Hell are real. What will your choice be?

You need to know that when Jesus says yes, no man can say no. Lay up for yourselves treasures in Heaven like it says in Matthew 6:19-21. Choose God and make Heaven your home. For greater is He that is in you than he that is in the world. Here's something to think about. Tell me, what would you do if Jesus knocked on your door

Here's a little encouragement to help you along the way. Just know God will always make a way. Psalms 121:1 says look to the hills from whence comes all your help; for behind every cloud, lies a ray of sunshine. Don't give up, press on with a smile. Live and let live each and every day. Remember you are God's child; and bright and fair your home in glory, one day is where you will stay. God knows and He cares. Your woes with no one He shares.

The three C's of life: Choices, Chances, and Changes. You must make a choice in order to take a chance or your life will never change. Make good choices today so you don't have regrets on tomorrow. Make your choices reflect your hopes, not your fears. Do your best to make the right ones and your best to learn from the wrong ones. We are responsible for the choices we make, but we also have to be willing to accept the consequences of those choices. For sometimes, the hardest decisions and the right decisions all turn out to be the same.

I come to tell you that there is liberty in knowing Jesus as your Savior. When the author of life speaks, where will you be? Hear God's voice today and make Him your choice. This is not our home, it's only temporary. There's something better awaiting. Our souls are being prepared for a new home; prepared for the Master's home on high. Are you ready? Whom will you choose? Tomorrow is not promised. Make your choice today. For what is seen is temporary, but what is unseen is eternal. The bottom line is that the road to eternity begins with and is paved with a choice.

Prayer:

Dear Lord, I know the choice is mine. Thank you for allowing me another opportunity to get it right. Please continue to be a fence all around me I ask. Help me to see and know thy will and live for you everyday. In Jesus name I pray amen.

Inspiring scriptures on choices:
Proverbs 16:9
The heart of a man plans his way, but the Lord establishes his steps.

Galatians 6:7-8
Do not be deceived: God is not mocked, for whatsoever one sows, that he will also reap. For the one who sows to his own flesh will from the flesh reap corruption, but the one who sows from the spirit will from the spirit reap eternal life.

Romans 6:13
For the wages of sin is death, but the gift of God is eternal life in Christ Jesus our lord.

2 Corinthians 5:7
For we walk by faith not by sight

Food for the soul:
Religion sets rules, Jesus sets us free.

Life's Little Recipe:

Lay up for yourselves treasures in Heaven. That's where the rewards lie.
For straight and narrow is the gate, to the great by and by.

Author Betty Hiner-Pickens

    I'm so proud to call Betty Pickens my mother. I've watched her work more than one job at a time to support me and my brother while pursuing one of her many dreams, putting herself through college, and graduated to go on to raise two boys into men. When I say I know she has amazingly strong faith, it's because I was by far not the greatest son I could have been. I talked back and got smacked lol...tried to be unruly and got my butt whipped!!! Then to top it off I just got out of prison and her faith never wavered. Through all of the tough times in our lives, I've watched her pray and never give up. She used to tell me it's OK to give in but never give up. She taught me to walk by faith and not by sight. She's about to accomplish another dream, she's written a book about faith and asked me to illustrate the cover.

    Mom I'm so proud of u ...God blessed me beyond measure with the greatest lady I could ever ask to be my mother... I love u and keep on water-walking.

                                                           Micheal Hiner